WELL, HELLO

MW01591211

I'm Angenett Curry, owner of PVS Financial Coaching & Services. We are a Personal Financial Literacy company who is on a mission to provide top quality financial education to help others improve their lifestyle. We use spiritual principles to guide our mission and vision. We would love to connect with you on Facebook and Instagram!

We wrote "Why Should I Manage My Money" to help encourage conversations with children about managing money and understanding why credit is so important. Our education system does not teach these fundamentals, so the conversations we have at home are even more vital for their adult success. Finances can be hard to explain to children, but we hope that this book helps guide the conversation in a way that makes "cents"! Teaching children the importance of credit is the key to furthering financial literacy in our communities.

Now, let's go meet Jase, the credit expert!

 @pvsfinancial   PVS Financial Coaching & Services

 www.prospectivevs.com    info@prospectivevs.com

Prospective Vision Solutions LLC

Hey, I'm Christopher! My family call me CJ.
I'm a 6th grader at Sherman Avenue
Elementary in Vicksburg, MS.
Did you know that you can have your own
savings account? My parents opened a savings
account in my name to deposit my monthly
allowances in.

Today at school we talked about how we spend our allowances. I was so excited because I wanted to tell my friends about my new savings account. You see, my parents told me that it's important to learn about money at a young age. I guess, grownups sometime have a problem with managing their money.

A savings account is a place in which you put the money that you want to save for future use. You see, a portion of my allowance is deposited into a savings account at my parent's bank. Not just any savings account though, it's called a high yield savings account. This means that the money my parents put in that account increases because it accumulates interest over time.

Interest is a percentage of money you earn by keeping your money in the high yield savings account. My mom says that the longer I let it stay there, the more money I make. The plan is to keep depositing a portion of my allowance every month until I become a grown up. Then, it will be my responsibility to continue to deposit money into the high yield savings account. By doing this, I will have money saved up for college, an apartment, or my first vehicle.

Of course, that doesn't take the place of investing. My parents purchase stocks, index and mutual funds to save money for when they get older. This account also accumulate interest just like the high yield savings account. My mom says that it accumulate more interest on certain ones. I will talk about this more in another book. Let's stick to the high yield savings account for now.

One thing that I have learned by watching my parents, adulthood is kind of tough. Dad says that you must plan your life while you're young. Make sure you build good credit by paying your bills on time. Dad also says that money make the world go round but good credit hold conversations. I don't know what that means but I know it's important for a grown up. I'll talk more about credit in another book.

My favorite sport is baseball. I guess being an adult is kind of like learning a new sport. You have to keep practicing until you get it right. My mom says that's why they are making sure that I have a head start. I have a high yield savings account, an investment account and I have a green dot debit card that I use to buy things with. I also give to charities like Le Bonheur Children's hospital and United Way.

Now back to high yield savings accounts. Make sure you do your research before opening your savings account. Some banks charge monthly fees . Most online banks offer free high yield savings accounts with higher interest rates than your local bank. The interst rate ranges from 30% - 75% which is about 10 times higher. Some also have a minimum deposit amount. This would be a great project for family time. You and your parents can research the banks together.

It's pretty easy to open a high yield savings account. All your parents need is your personal information like your social security number, date of birth, your address and phone number. They would also need to create an account online and then complete some paperwork to confirm the account. This can be done on their cell phone, tablet or computer. Ask them if you could watch so you can see how it's done.

Once the account is created, they will have to deposit money into the account. You can deposit 10 or 20% of your allowance. It is totally up to you. The more you deposit, the more interest your account will build. I deposit 20% of my monthly allowance into my high yield savings account. I've had my account for about four months now and it's already building interest. When the statement comes in the mail, my parents show it to me so I can understand what's going on.

Now it's time to figure out ways you can get extra allowances. Talk with your parents and see if there's anything you can do to raise your allowance amount. Ask to wash the car, pick leaves out the yard, or help mommy with her chores. You can also ask your Grandparents, Aunt or Uncle to mow their lawn, pick up trash in the yard or clean out the dog house. Ask your friends and family to give cash instead of buying gifts for birthdays and holidays.

Here are some important things to remember about high yield savings accounts:
1. They build more interest than regular savings accounts.
2. Online accounts usually don't charge fees,
3. The more you deposit, the more interest builds.
4. Your parent's have to open the account for you.
5. Try to figure out ways to earn extra cash to deposit into your account.

There was a lot to discuss on savings accounts. This is definitely something to sit down and discuss with your parents. It was a lot for me at first but now since I've been saving for a while, it all make sense. I am currently saving 20% of my allowance because I don't have any bills to pay but when I become an adult, I may have to save 10% until I get familiar with paying my bills.

It's totally up to you how much you want to save. The goal is to start saving something. Never spend the money you save and give yourself a yearly goal to reach. If you want to be a responsible adult, it starts now. Just imagine how much money you could save up in the next 10 years.

Thanks for hanging out with me today. I really enjoyed your company. Remember to have a conversation with your parents and family members on doing extra chores around the house to increase your allowance. I've learned to master my finances by putting my money into things that will give me more money. What about you? What have you learned by reading this book?

How to apply the principles in this book to real life:

Let's say you get $20 a week for allowances. You take the $20 and split in in half. The first $10 goes to your Greenlight card. The second half is then split in three ways. You take $4 and deposit into your savings and $4 is deposited into your Stockpile investment account, then the last $2 you can give to a needy cause like donating it to United Way, Le Bonheur Children Hospital or just buying a friend a burger. Your parents can do this for you until they teach you how to transfer the amounts from your Greenlight card to your savings and investment accounts. All you do is repeat this every time you get your allowance. Whatever is left on your Greenlight card is yours to spend. It's just that easy!

- Talk to your parents about giving you an weekly allowance

- Make a chore list and ask parent to put a dollar amount on each chore.

- Get paid and deposit your allowance as described on the previous page.

- Repeat the steps every time you get your allowance.

Repeat, please

WEEKLY CHORE CHART

CHORES:	M	T	W	T	F	S	S
_____	☐	☐	☐	☐	☐	☐	☐
_____	☐	☐	☐	☐	☐	☐	☐
_____	☐	☐	☐	☐	☐	☐	☐
_____	☐	☐	☐	☐	☐	☐	☐
_____	☐	☐	☐	☐	☐	☐	☐
_____	☐	☐	☐	☐	☐	☐	☐
_____	☐	☐	☐	☐	☐	☐	☐
_____	☐	☐	☐	☐	☐	☐	☐
_____	☐	☐	☐	☐	☐	☐	☐
_____	☐	☐	☐	☐	☐	☐	☐

LET'S DO THIS!

ALLOWANCE INFO SHEET

1. Save

Allowance

* .20 =

20%

2. Invest

Allowance

* .20 =

20%

3. Give

Allowance

* .10 =

10%

4. Spend

Allowance

* .50 =

50%

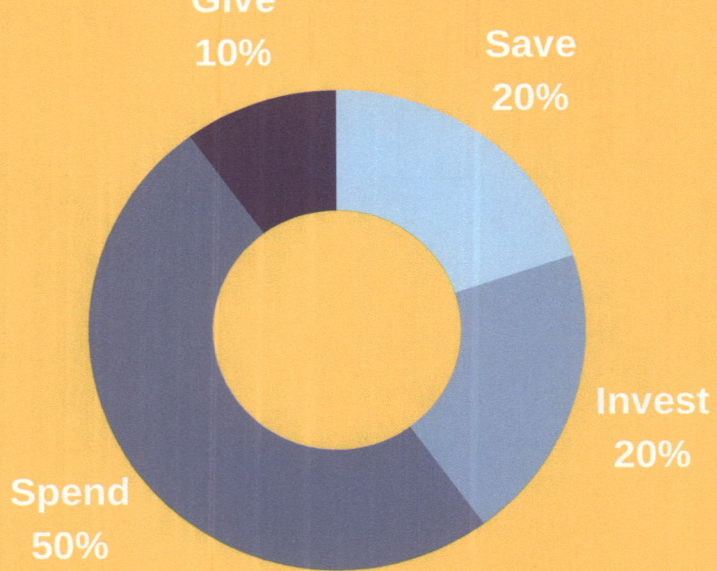

Give
10%

Save
20%

Invest
20%

Spend
50%

Allowance: $20.00

Save 20% = $4.00

Invest 20% = $4.00

Give 10% = $2.00

Spend 50% = $10.00

SAVINGS

WHAT ARE YOU SAVING FOR?

Instructions: Figure out your weekly percentages to reach your goal.

Week #	Week #	Week #	Week #
1.	1.	1.	1.
2.	2.	2.	2.
3.	3.	3.	3.
4.	4.	4.	4.

Week #	Week #	Week #	Week #
1.	1.	1.	1.
2.	2.	2.	2.
3.	3.	3.	3.
4.	4.	4.	4.

My Goal:

WORD SEARCH

Circle words in the puzzle below

```
C H O R E E V A S
S A C R E D I T P
U L M O N E Y R E
G U S N A B S B N
I N V E S T C I D
V A T M A A O T U
E R U C R M R T R
Z G R N R A E Y Y
B U R E A U E R W
```

invest   give   earn   car
debt   spend   score   money
credit   bureau   save   chore